Read Write Inc.

Literacy and Language
Pupils' Book

4

Janey Pursglove and **Charlotte Raby**

Series developed by **Ruth Miskin**

OXFORD
UNIVERSITY PRESS

OXFORD
UNIVERSITY PRESS

Great Clarendon Street, Oxford, OX2 6DP,
United Kingdom

Oxford University Press is a department of the
University of Oxford. It furthers the University's
objective of excellence in research, scholarship,
and education by publishing worldwide.
Oxford is a registered trade mark of Oxford University
Press in the UK and in certain other countries

British Library Cataloguing in Publication Data
Data available

ISBN: 978-0-19-833079-0

10 9 8 7 6 5 4 3 2 1

Paper used in the production of this book is a natural,
recyclable product made from wood grown in sustainable
forests. The manufacturing process conforms to the
environmental regulations of the country of origin.

Printed in China by Imago

Acknowledgements

Cover illustration by Chuck Groenink

Illustrations by: Laura Anderson; Leo Broadley; Lee Cosgrove;
Clare Elsom; Katie May Green; Chuck Groenick; Alejandro
O'Keeffe; Andrew Painter; Q2A; Andrés Martínez Ricci;
Yannick Robert; Ariel Sela; David Semple; Anthony Trimmer

The publishers would like to thank the following for
the permission to reproduce photographs: **p10t**: UbjsP/
Shutterstock; **p10b**: Anton Petrus/Shutterstock; **p11l**: Click
Bestsellers/Shutterstock; **p11r**: silver tiger/Shutterstock;
p12: Piti Tan/Shutterstock; **p13t**: Theo Malings/Shutterstock;
p13b: Eliks/Shutterstock; **p15** clockwise from top right: Stu
Porter/Shutterstock; CreativeNature.nl/Shutterstock; djgis/
Shutterstock; Giovanni Benintende/Shutterstock; **p17t**:
anaken2012/Shutterstock; **p17b**: Mike Liu/Shutterstock; **p19**:
oorka/Shutterstock; **p21**: Memo Angeles/Shutterstock; **p23l**:
Eric Isselee/Shutterstock; **p23r**: Joel Blit/Shutterstock; **p28**:
Mark III Photonics/Shutterstock; **p41**: dedMazay/Shutterstock;
p43l: Undergroundarts.co.uk/Shutterstock; **p43r**: SusIO/
Shutterstock; **p44**: Oliver Hoffmann/Shutterstock; **p53**: Ales
Liska/Shutterstock; **p59**: Balthasar Thomass/Alamy; **p64l**: Ed
Isaacs/Shutterstock; **p64m**: swinner/Shutterstock; **p64r**: Eric
Isselee/Shutterstock

TEACHERS:
For inspirational support plus
free resources and eBooks
www.oxfordprimary.co.uk

PARENTS:
Help your child's learning
with essential tips, phonics
support and free eBooks
www.oxfordowl.co.uk

Contents

Lost or Stolen?

Reading

① Read a story version 3

Discuss these questions with your partner.

A Why do you think Taj's parents work such long hours?

B How do you think Taj feels about going to his cousins' house almost every day in the holidays?

C How do you think Chandra feels about Ravi's behaviour towards Taj?

D How would you describe Taj's behaviour?

② Who changes most?

Read the section of *Lost or Stolen?* from "My parents were going to take me..." (line 3, page 11) to "I wish I had a sister" (line 6, page 12). Then read these statements and decide whether Taj, Chandra or Ravi has changed the most.

A Taj shows his true feelings here instead of just showing off and boasting.

B Chandra was really irritated by Taj at the beginning, but now she is kind and gives him a *rakhi*.

C Ravi was jealous of Taj and was going to accuse Taj of theft, but here he feels sorry for him.

③ Text detectives

Can you explain this diagram to your partner?

Writing on a page

The page

'Secret' writing

Now match sentences A, B and C from *Lost or Stolen?* with 'secret' writing sentences 1, 2 and 3.

From *Lost or Stolen?*

A Chandra and Ravi were extremely relieved when Taj's dad arrived to collect him.

B "I know Taj can be hard work," Mum said, "but be kind to him. He's not as fortunate as you two."

C Ravi sighed heavily. Taj's parents had loads of money and gave him whatever he wanted – the newest, the best and the most expensive of *everything*.

'Secret' writing

1 I feel sorry that the children had to put up with Taj's behaviour, but they don't realise how lucky they are compared to Taj!

2 Taj had been really irritating and they couldn't wait for him to go.

3 Ravi thought his cousin was very spoilt, but at the same time he was really envious.

④ What if not…?

Discuss these What if not…? questions.

A What if not *Ravi's dad who borrowed the games console*? What if *Taj had borrowed it without asking permission*?

B What if not *Taj that Chandra gave the spare rakhi to*? What if *she had given it to someone else*?

C What if not *silent about the missing games console*? What if *Ravi had accused Taj of stealing it to his face*?

⑤ Hidden conversations

Taj has everything he could wish for, except for time with his mum and dad. Imagine what would happen if he told his parents he wished they would spend more time with him.

Discuss:

★ how Taj would begin the conversation

★ whether his parents would listen or say they were too busy

★ what Taj would say about how he feels and what he wants.

Would Taj's mum and dad:

★ think he was spoilt and be angry with him?

★ feel sad that they hadn't realised that Taj was lonely?

★ not understand and offer to buy him more things?

Make notes for a role-play between Taj and one of his parents.

Writing

① What would you do?

Oliver and Samya are playing a dilemmas game. The dilemma is this: as a sports captain, you have to pick team members. Your best friend is hopeless at sport but is desperate to play in the team. Do you pick your friend or not?

Partner 1 is Samya and Partner 2 is Oliver. Read the speech bubbles aloud.

If I didn't pick my friend, they might fall out with me.

If they are a true friend, they would understand.

It could be their only chance to play in a team.

But I would want the team to win, so that would be hard luck!

I would rather lose a game of football than a friend. I would pick my mate – every time.

I wouldn't. A captain has to think of the team, not her friends!

Now discuss with your partner which action *you* would take if you had this dilemma.

② Dramatic reconstruction

The children have arrived home very late from the fair. They have to face Ravi and Chandra's mum, who is angry and upset. Their dad has gone back to the fair to look for them.

Partner 1s you are Ravi or Mum.

Partner 2s you are Taj or Chandra.

Develop and practise a short role-play of the scene. Think about who will be feeling:

angry	guilty	relieved	betrayed
scared	upset	anxious	sulky
sorry	regretful	defiant	disappointed

③ Grammar: inverted commas

Take turns to read the extracts below. Discuss which ones show *direct speech* and which ones show *reported speech*.

A Jake ran up to the toy shop window. "Please can I have that one?" he asked.

B Zena told her mum that she was looking forward to going to the fair.

C "I can't wait to go swimming after school," said Luca.

D Sophia's dad said that she couldn't go to the park until it had stopped raining.

④ Write a story 3

You are on a trip to the fair with Ravi, Chandra and Taj. Turn the pictures in your head into words to describe the experience. Choose a variety of powerful words, including:

★ *verbs* – I *clutched* the sides of the Big Wheel carriage as we started to move.

★ *adjectives* – I clutched the sides of the *swaying* Big Wheel carriage as we started to move.

★ *adverbs* – I clutched the sides of the swaying Big Wheel carriage as we *slowly* started to move.

Remember to think about what you:

| see | hear | smell | taste | feel |

Say your sentences aloud before you write them down.

① Grammar: word classes and suffixes

Use your dictionary to look up these words:

| noun | verb | adjective | adverb |

Now close your dictionary!

Partner 1 choose two of the words above and explain to your partner what they mean.

Partner 2 tell Partner 1 if you think this is the right definition.

Then swap over.

Did you know there are different kinds of nouns?

★ **Proper nouns** are the names of particular places or people, and important things like days of the week.

★ **Collective nouns** describe a group of things.

★ **Abstract nouns** are things we can't see or touch, like feelings or ideas.

Which kinds of nouns are these?

A a flock of birds

B terror, joy, wisdom

C January, New York

Check in your dictionary for any that you are not sure about.

② Write 1

Read this email from the editor of *Gadget Magic* **magazine with your partner.**

To: Staff

Subject: Article – urgent!

Good morning team,

I need a short article for page 10 of next month's magazine on a gadget of the future called 'SPEC-tacular'. I'm attaching a mind map to show you the main information about the gadget. I want you to use this to create a fun, informative article that will appeal to our young readers.

Try to:

- write in the same style as that fabulous feature, The Greatest Gadget of Them All, presented as a story about someone who has this gadget
- include a lot of information from the mind map
- persuade readers what a great gadget it would be.

Remember to read your work through before you send it to me – I don't like lots of mistakes!

Good luck.

Ed

Use the tips in the email and the information in the mind map to write your article for the *Gadget Magic* **magazine editor.**

③ **Write 2**

Use the prompts below to help you create an advice and information leaflet about keeping your phone safe.

⭑ Advice could be sorted into *Dos* and *Don'ts*. These would be commands, e.g. *Don't show off your new phone.*

⭑ Have a separate section for key information with subheadings. These could be questions, e.g. *What are the facts?*

⭑ Bullet points are useful to list advice or information in no particular order – just like the ones in these prompts!

⭑ Numbered points can be used instead, especially if you want the prompts to be read in a particular order.

⭑ Remember to have a title or main heading. It should make it clear what the leaflet is about.

> Boxes are also useful to make a special fact or point stand out from the rest of the text.

④ Write 3

Take turns to read the information about Holo-World on the board.

Discuss what other features Holo-World could have to make it even more special. Write your ideas down in your Daily log and keep them a secret until your presentation!

Then plan your presentation with your partner.

A Decide what each of you will focus on and say.

B Think about how you will explain what the product will look like – you could use pictures or diagrams.

C Plan in some time for the panel to ask questions at the end. Make sure you think about what questions they might ask and what your answers will be!

Remember these Top Tips for presentations. Make sure you:

★ speak slowly and clearly

★ sound excited about the product

★ look at your audience when you are speaking.

Poetry

Reading

1 Special phrases

Partner 1 read the Special phrases with lots of expression.

Partner 2 read the effects.

Special phrase from 'At the End of a School Day'	Effect
…bag-swinging, shouting children.	The **rhythm** of the words matches the rhythm of the swinging bags. It helps to create a strong picture.
…carries the creature to the safety of a shady hedge.	The **alliteration** of the /k/ sound in *carries* and *creature* makes you slow down as you read the words. It shows that the creature was carried slowly and carefully.
Girl, children, sky and sun hold their breath.	The use of the **list** here shows that everyone and everything are watching and waiting – all caring about the hedgehog at the same moment.

Discuss which Special phrase is your favourite and why.

② Read a poem

Discuss these questions with your partner.

A Why do you think the children were 'bag-swinging' and 'shouting' as they came down the drive?

B What images appear in your mind when you hear the lines: 'Deafened, the sky winces. / The sun gapes in surprise.' ?

C When the hedgehog has been placed under the 'shady hedge', why is everyone silent for a moment? What might they be thinking?

③ Daily log: similes

Take turns to look at a picture and complete a simile. Remember that similes use *as* or *like*.

For example:

As swift **as a** hunter.

Graceful **like a** cheetah.

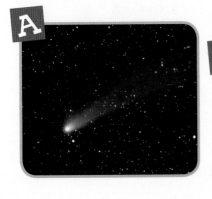

④ Form 2

Think of some words that rhyme with the words below.

| trees | trick | sheep |

Then choose words to complete these rhyming couplets.

A I love my cat, my cat loves trees,

But my poor cat has lots of …

B I want to teach you all a trick,

Look at the cards, which one will you …

C At the farm I saw some sheep,

I count them as I fall …

Writing

1 **What do you think?**

Read the different versions of the stanza.

1 I dump my bag
and gingerly, so gingerly
I tiptoe away from the creature
who stares at me with eyes like yellow stones.

2 I clutch my bag
and cautiously, so cautiously
I tiptoe towards the creature
who watches me with eyes like burning suns.

3 I dump my fear
and gently, so gently
I stroke the creature
who looks at me with eyes like a frightened child's.

Now discuss these questions.

A Which version sounds the most powerful when you hear it aloud?

B Which word do you think is the most effective at describing how
the creature is approached: *gingerly,
cautiously* or *gently*?

C Is it more interesting to say *I dump my bag*
or *I dump my fear*?

D Which simile about the creature's
eyes is your favourite? Why?

② Write a poem 3

Discuss the questions with your partner. Use the prompts to help you begin writing your new stanza.

A What do I want my audience to think and feel?
Do I want them to laugh or feel sad, scared or thoughtful?

B How can I create some clear, strong images?
Should I add a simile, or use powerful words and phrases?

C How can I create a strong shape on the page?
Should I follow the pattern of versions 1, 2 and 3 or create a different pattern?

D Do I want my stanza to rhyme?
Should I have rhyming words at the end of the lines or words that rhyme within a line?

① Grammar: paragraphs

Take turns to read a paragraph each of the Anthology text 'Your Alien Experiences'. Read the summary of the first two paragraphs below.

Strange happenings

Miss J.L. was napping on the sofa when she was suddenly abducted by aliens. She was carried away to a white room full of switches and flashing lights. On a screen she saw Earth disappearing!

Work with your partner to summarise the next three paragraphs in your Anthology under the appropriate subheadings. Record your summaries in your Daily log.

| An alien encounter | Questions, questions… | Back to reality |

② **Write 2**

Take turns to read this email from the editor of *The Sentinel*.

To: journalist.team.thesentinel@newsmail.con

Subject: Escaped lion report

Dear team,

Please read the attached notes from a reporter about a case of an escaped lion. Can you turn them into an interesting report? I'll use the best ones in the newspaper and on our website.

I want:

- the facts please – Who was involved? What happened? Why? Where? When?
- a couple of good quotes from the recounts of those involved
- a short article – we don't have room for a long piece
- a serious tone – it is a serious topic and we are a serious newspaper.

I **do not** want:

- opinion – let our readers know the facts and think for themselves
- exaggeration – don't make the situation sound more dramatic than it really is.

Many thanks,
Karen Green

The Sentinel

Escaped lion on the run

A lion was reported missing from Brooklands Hall Safari Park.

Now use these reporter's notes and eyewitness accounts to write your report.

Reporter's notes:

- Brooklands Hall Safari Park missing a lion
- hole in wire fencing spotted
- could have been missing for days
- staff upset as he is a favourite
- will be hungry and favours uncooked meat
- should not be approached
- reward for information.

Eyewitness accounts:

Lady Catherine Eccles, owner of the Safari Park:

"I am very upset. We have to take the blame, so I will personally give a £500 reward for information that helps us to catch Lenny before he hurts himself or anyone else!"

Ben York and Josie Grey, animal carers at the Safari Park:

Ben: "I check the fences twice a week. Someone must have cut the hole in the fence!"

Josie: "I just want Lenny back safe and sound. He is my favourite lion at the park."

PC Thomas Hughes, Investigating Officer:

"The public must be protected. We are talking to police in nearby Clifton who are investigating reports of a lion in a school playground. If you spot the lion, please do not approach it – leave it to the experts!"

③ Role-play

Partner 1 is a reporter from the *Gossip Gazette*.

Partner 2 is a child who was in the playground when the lion appeared.

Prompts

Reporter:

★ Remember, you want a sensational story so you might encourage the child to exaggerate a bit!

★ Ask who the child is, what happened, where they were standing, whether they were scared and what everyone else was doing.

Child:

★ Remember, you might be tempted to exaggerate how close you came to the lion. Or, you may have genuinely found the experience terrifying.

★ What did you think was going to happen? Were you scared? Were you a hero?

Now change roles.

Partner 1 is a teacher who was in the playground when the lion appeared.

Partner 2 is a reporter from the *Gossip Gazette.*

Prompts

Teacher:

★ Remember, you might not want parents to think that their children were in danger so you might try to hide what happened. Or you might want everyone to see you as a hero!

★ What did you do to keep the children safe? What did you think might happen? Were you frightened?

Reporter:

★ Remember, you want a sensational story so you might encourage the teacher to exaggerate a bit!

★ Ask the teacher what happened, what they did to protect the children and whether they were frightened.

The Bogey Men
and the
Trolls Next Door

Reading

1 Daily log

Share what you know about the story so far with your partner. Discuss:

★ the names of the two families

★ where they live

★ the main events (things that have happened) so far.

Now draw a mind map with these branches and headings:

Families   Where they live

The story

Main events

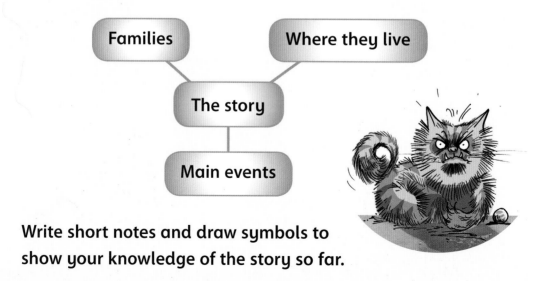

Write short notes and draw symbols to show your knowledge of the story so far.

② Respond and predict

Discuss the questions below.

A How do you think Fred the Bogeyman should have behaved towards Dave the Troll when they met?

B What do you think the catastrophe might be? Who or what might be involved?

C Are the families likely to become friends or stay enemies forever?

D Do you think the Bogey Bog is important to the story? Why?

③ Read a story version 3

Discuss the questions below.

A If you had to live with the Bogeys or the Trolls, which would you prefer and why?

B What did you think had happened to the babies when they disappeared?

C The story is written in rhyming verses. How does this change the way you read it?

(4) **Word power**

Partner 1 read the word and its meaning.
Partner 2 read the sentence containing the word.

★ **fateful** – very important, often in a disastrous way
It was a *fateful* day when the princess pricked her finger on
the spinning wheel – now she would sleep for 100 years!

★ **indignant** – annoyed, outraged
I felt very *indignant* when I was blamed for breaking a vase,
because it was the dog!

★ **desolate** – bleak and depressing
The cold, gloomy hillside was a *desolate* place in the dusk.

★ **destination** – place of arrival, journey's end
Our holiday *destination* was sunny Cornwall!

**Challenge your partner to use at least two of the Power words
this week. Write the Power words in your Daily log. Check you
have the correct spellings.**

1 Points of view

Discuss the questions below.

A Is Fred being truthful when he says he avoids 'stress and strife'? Why?

B What could have happened to Fred to make him so anti-Troll at the beginning of the story?

C What do you think Dave and Dolly thought about Fred's behaviour when they first moved in next door? What do *you* think about it?

D Some people are afraid of those who are different. Could Fred have been a little scared of the Troll family? Why?

2 What if not...?

Discuss these What if not...? questions.

A What if not *Fred the Bogeyman narrating*? What if *someone else had narrated the story*?

B What if not *Trolls*? What if *another Bogey family had moved in next door*?

③ **Write a story 1**

The older Troll and Bogey children have formed a band and started rehearsing.

Read these notes from a writer's log book with your partner. They are a plan for a story about the band.

> - Something goes wrong – could be with equipment or band member.
>
> - Where is it taking place? Is it a party? A concert? An audition?
>
> - Could have someone or something that comes to the rescue.
>
> - Been asked to play in front of an audience for first time.

Discuss and decide the order of the notes to make a bare bones story structure.

④ Daily log

Help Beryl Bogey to finish the chorus for her love song to Fred.
Read her ideas and discuss which lines you think are the best.

1st line: Oh Fred, Oh Fred, I love you,

2nd line: You're…

Beryl's ideas for the 2nd line:

- my bogey heart's delight
- more gorgeous than Brad Pott
- so handsome (in my view)

3rd line: Oh Fred, Oh Fred, I love you,

4th line: Even…

Beryl's ideas for the 4th line:

- though your vest's too tight
- though you don't look right
- more than I love Snot
- when you've lost the plot
- more than bogey stew
- more each day, it's true!

5 Grammar: adverbials

Take turns to read each sentence about the families.
The adverbial is circled in each sentence.

★ A knock came on the Bogey's door (one fateful evening.)

★ Fred the Bogeyman greeted Dave the Troll (with a bad, bogey sneer.)

★ Baby Bogey blew bubbles (in the sunny garden.)

For each sentence, decide whether the adverbial tells us *how*,
when, or *where* something happened.

Now take turns to read the sentences below. Discuss which part
of each sentence is the adverbial. If you are not sure, work out
which part tells you *how*, *when* or *where* something happened.

A The Bogeys dumped their rubbish on the Troll family's lawn.

B One sunny morning, both babies disappeared!

C Worn out to a frazzle, the families reached the Bogey Bog.

D The babies were having fun in the mud.

E From that moment on, the families became friends.

① Audience and purpose

Think about what you saw on the Stellar Stage School website and discuss the questions below.

★ What kind of school is yours? Stage school? Sports academy? Both?

★ What age range is it for?

★ What are you going to call it?

★ Can you think of a great slogan to encourage people to apply?

Discuss the questions below to help you plan your website.

A What is the purpose of the website?

B Who is likely to look at it? Think about:

- pupils already at the school

- children who want to find out about the school

- parents.

C What do you want on the home page?

D What do you want on the second page?

E What information and instructions are important?

Make notes in your Daily log.

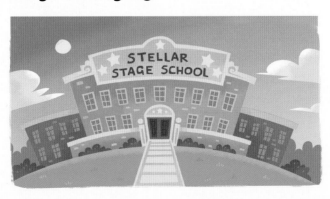

② Deconstruction 1

A stage school hopeful tells our expert, Miss Lark, why he'd be perfect for the Stellar Stage School. Let's see what she thinks!

Partner 1 read the pupil's speech bubbles.

Partner 2 read Miss Lark's responses.

> I WILL be a Stellar Stage School super star! I am already AMAZING at everything!

> Well, we would have to see what you can really do at an audition. Remember, though – we are looking for people who are willing to learn, not ready-made stars! You need to be prepared to learn from our experts.

> But stage school's an easy road to fame and fortune, right? I'd give it a go as long as it's not too much hard work – I mean, I need enough hours in the day to fit in my computer games and football practice…

> I don't think stage school is right for you, young man! It's very hard work and there's no guaranteed success at the end.

③ Write 3

You are going to teach pupils how to get the pop star look!
Here are Miss Lark's Top Tips for how to be a good teacher:

⭐ Sound confident – even if you don't feel it!

⭐ Use different ways to explain something:

- a picture or diagram

- props

- talk, but not for too long and do not mumble

- write a few key points on a handout to give to pupils.

⭐ Make sure you have lots of good advice to share with your pupils.
Here are a few ideas:

experiment with different styles

copy a favourite pop star

give old clothes a makeover

create your own publicity shots

get a cool new haircut

The Fly and the Fool

> **Reading**

① Read a script version 3

Discuss the questions below.

A Which character do you like the most and why?

B Do you think it's right that Mr Lo makes a profit when he loans money to other people? Why?

C Do you think Lan was clever to use riddles to trick Mr Lo? Why?

D Who do you think was the most honourable character in the play and why?

② Think and link

Look at the story map with your partner. Discuss the questions.

A Where does the story start?

B Why must Lan's family borrow money from Mr Lo?

C How long do they need it for?

D What happens when Lan's family try to pay Mr Lo back?

E Mr Lo comes to visit Lan's family. Why is this visit so important?

F Where is the final part of the play set? Who does the Judge decide is right?

③ Most important?

**What is the most important moment in the whole play?
Take turns to read these statements. Discuss which statement
you agree with, and why.**

A The most important moment
is when the Judge makes his
decision at the end of the play.

B The most important moment is
when the fly witnesses the deal.

C When Lan tempts Mr Lo into
guessing his riddle he saves
his family, so that is the most
important moment.

D The most important moment
of the play is when Kym and
Lan's family take out the loan,
otherwise there would be
no play.

1 What if not...?

Discuss these What if not...? questions.

A What if not *fair*? What if *the Judge took sides with one of the characters?*

B What if not *the right decision*? What if *the Judge got it wrong*?

C What if not *this folk tale*? What if *a character from another traditional tale was on trial*?

2 Show, don't tell

Discuss how to turn this *telling* extract into two or three *showing* sentences. Remember, characters show what they are thinking by how they talk, the expressions on their faces and how they move.

In the morning, the King stared at the huge room filled to the brim with gold. Greed filled his heart and he said, "Tomorrow you will spin another room of straw into gold and then you can be my wife, or else... you die."

③ Stage directions

Read this part of the script of *Rumpelstiltskin* in groups of three.

A large room containing a spinning wheel and a huge pile of straw. It is dimly lit and looks shabby and cold.

Bethany is standing in the middle of the stage, lit by moonlight streaming in from a small, barred window. She is hugging her arms around herself. The King is standing just inside the door, looking imposing. Rumpelstiltskin is crouching in the shadows in a corner. He looks delighted.

King   *(Sternly)* Now you will spin another room of straw into gold and then you will be my wife, or else...you die.

Rumpelstiltskin   *(Whispering to the audience)* Ah! Now my plan has come together perfectly! She has nothing left to give me for my magic. I shall get what I've always wanted.

King   *(Strutting towards the door)* Well girl, get on with it! The sooner you spin the straw into gold, the sooner you will be my wife. Stop dawdling.

The door slams and Bethany begins to shake and cry.

Bethany   Oh, how can I do what he wants? The clever goblin is the one who has the magic, not me. *(She falls to her knees and cries.)* And I have nothing to give him now.

Rumpelstiltskin creeps up behind the sobbing girl and gently taps her on the shoulder. Then he gives the audience a knowing wink.

Rumpelstiltskin Poor Bethany. Why are you shut in this dark, dank cell? Have you been ordered to spin that enormous pile of straw into gold? *(Aside to the audience)* Just ask me…and then you will have to grant me my dearest wish.

Bethany Oh dear, sweet goblin. You are right, I have to spin the straw into gold or I will die. Will you help me? I have nothing to give you.

Rumpelstiltskin *(With a devious smile)* I will help you if you will give me…your first-born child.

Bethany stares at the goblin in horror. Lights fade to black.

Discuss these questions with your partner.

A What is the setting of the play?

B How are the characters speaking?

C How are the characters moving?

D What props are needed for this part of the play?

Write your findings in your Daily log.

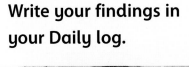

4 Write a script 2

Use the prompts below to help you continue to write your scene.

★ Make sure you include stage directions.

★ Use the dialogue and stage directions to show how the characters think, move and speak.

★ Make sure you include an interruption from another character and the Judge or the King's response.

★ Think carefully about the style in which the characters speak and the words they might use.

5 Write a script 3

Use the instructions to help you write a speech in which the King, who is on trial, pleads with the Judge to let him go.

★ The King needs to say sorry for what he did.

★ He needs to show that he knows exactly what he did and how it hurt others.

★ Then he tries to blame Rumpelstiltskin for what happened.

★ Finally, use the King's secret as a reason for what he did, to show that he was not just being cruel, greedy and heartless.

1 Word power

Partner 1 read the word and its meaning.
Partner 2 read the sentence containing
the word.

★ **committed** – carried out, done
The judge said the man was guilty – he
had clearly *committed* the crime.

★ **victim** – a person harmed as a result of a crime
The *victim* had to be very brave when she identified who
had stolen her handbag.

★ **reconstruction** – acting out a past event
The class watched a *reconstruction* of life on board
a Tudor ship.

★ **suspect** – a person thought to have committed a crime
The *suspect* looked very worried when
the policeman produced two pictures
of her in the bank.

② Grammar: plurals, possession and apostrophes

Take it in turns to read these sentences, then discuss and decide which bold word is correct in each sentence.

A There were **nettles/nettle's/nettles'** growing by the footpath.

B The **girls/girl's/girls'** changing rooms were being cleaned while they were swimming.

C That **rabbits/rabbit's/rabbits'** hutch is much too small for it.

D Katie borrowed **Jakes/Jake's/Jakes'** coloured pencils.

E The naughty dog ate all of the **biscuits/biscuit's/biscuits'**.

F The **houses/house's/houses'** roofs were blown off in the storm.

③ Write 2

Use the following prompts to guide you when assessing your evidence and planning your writing.

Introduction

★ Say what type of evidence you have chosen, e.g. DNA, an interview, a photograph.

★ Say where the evidence came from and why you have chosen it.

Evidence 1 and 2

★ Start with the strongest piece of evidence.

★ Break down, in clear steps, how your evidence was collected, so the reader can see it is reliable.

★ Show where there may be problems with your evidence. Be clear about why there could be doubt.

★ Include technical language, if appropriate.

Conclusion

★ What makes your evidence reliable?

★ How does it prove that the criminal is guilty?

Runaways!

Reading

① Grammar: standard English

Take turns to read the sentences. Decide which of the words in bold should be used to turn the sentences into standard English.

A The three girls **was/were** walking to school together.

B Could you pass **them/those** sweets over please?

C I knew he **was/were** very good at drawing.

D My brother **did/done** his homework this morning but I haven't done mine yet.

② Special phrases

Take turns to read the Special phrases with your partner. Share what images you think of as you read each one.

his body shaking distressingly	a bolt of fear
looked at her suspiciously	questioning look

③ Character

Discuss the questions with your partner.

A Do you think Mr Patch is a kind man?

B How you think Mr Patch behaves towards other people?

C How does Mr Patch feel about Hannah and John?

D Does Mr Patch think he is important? Does he think that Hannah and John are important?

Write a paragraph in your Daily log to describe Mr Patch.

④ Summarising the story

Discuss the questions with your partner.
Plan your trailer in your Daily log.

A What are the three most important or interesting moments in the story?

B How will you introduce the characters?

C What questions or statements could you use to draw the audience in?

D What cliff-hanger will you use to end the trailer?

Writing

① What if not...?

Discuss these What if not...? questions.

A What if not *mean spirited*? What if *Mr Patch were a caring workhouse master*?

B What if not *saved*? What if *Dr Barnardo hadn't helped Hannah and John*?

C What if not *set in the past*? What if *two children ran away from home today*?

② Build a character

Read the descriptions of Hannah and John written by Matron. Discuss with your partner any thoughts you have about Matron.

Name: John Williams   Date: 23 November 1882

Appearance: A tiny boy, well below the size I'd expect for an eight-year-old. He is caked in mud. His clothes are threadbare but well kept. His eyes are huge with fear — poor mite. He has a terrible infection and I can only hope it is not tuberculosis or pneumonia.

Other comments: The boy is very thin and weak. John will need constant care if he is to fully recover.

Recommendations: Once well, John will need to build up his strength. He is liable to get ill again if we don't get a good layer of fat on him. We will assess him later and see if he is able to learn to read and write.

Name: Hannah Williams   Date: 23 November 1882

Appearance: Pitifully thin, trembling with tiredness, covered in mud, ragged clothes but well kept. Some health problems (most likely caused by a poor diet).

Other comments: Hannah seems desperate to stay with her brother. The first thing she did on arrival was to feed him. She is constantly looking around and is very scared of any sudden noises or movements. I fear both Hannah and her brother have been poorly treated.

Recommendations: Firstly, we must make Hannah feel safe and get her fed. She should learn to read as soon as possible. She should also learn some skills that will give her safe employment. We shall start with needlework.

Use the prompts to help you to write some dialogue for Matron as she tells Dr Barnardo about Hannah.

Prompts

★ What is the most important thing that Matron will want to tell Dr Barnardo about Hannah?

★ How will Matron describe Hannah's appearance when she arrived?

★ What does Matron think Hannah needs?

③ Build a story 3

Take turns to read sections of the story.

The children trudged along Stepney Causeway. The tall, industrial buildings made the road seem grey and tired. Hannah kept muttering to herself and John held onto her tightly, wheezing as he walked. The road seemed so long and forbidding that Hannah began to wonder if they had come to the right place.

They plodded on despondently. They came to a huge railway bridge, dark and sooty from the steam trains. They were about to give up when Hannah looked up and saw the sign for the shelter.

Warily, the two children went up the steps and stood in front of the enormous, shiny black door. Hannah sighed. The knocker was almost out of her reach but she stretched up and lifted it. She released it from her fingers and flinched as it thudded against the solid door.

A moment later, the door swung silently open and a smartly uniformed woman stood in front of them. She smiled down at the children and then a small frown appeared on her face. "Come inside, you look exhausted," she said.

John looked questioningly at Hannah. Hannah explained to the woman that they had been told to come by Dr Barnardo.

"Come in, come in," she insisted. "I am the matron here at the Shelter. We are a refuge for destitute children. No child is ever turned away," she reassured them.

Matron took John by the hand and led him and Hannah up the stairs. They turned a corner and saw a huge room filled with beds.

"This is the San," said Matron. "You will stay here until you are both well. These nurses will look after you." And with a tight smile she left the two children staring into the room in awe.

The nurses all wore clean, white uniforms. Two of them helped Hannah and John wash and get dressed in clean clothes. Hannah was delighted to feel clean. She looked over at John, who shivered distressingly as he was cleaned and dressed. At last the children were given delicious hot food to eat.

Later that evening, when Hannah was clean and rested, Matron came back to speak to her. "Your brother is very poorly," she explained. "We need to give him constant care and build up his strength. You can still see him but I want you to learn to read and sew. It is important that you are able to work one day, Hannah."

Hannah returned to her bed and crawled under the sheets. She tossed and turned, thoughts and ideas rushing through her head. She could hear voices at the bottom of the stairs. Hannah tried hard to block them out, but then she heard her brother's name.

Text by Charlotte Raby

Use the questions below to evaluate the story.

A How does the author *show* rather than *tell* how Hannah and John are feeling? Try to give some examples.

B Which words or phrases did you like?

C How did the description and the historical references help you to imagine that you were there?

D Are you excited to learn what happens next? Why?

④ Write a story 1

Read the prompts with your partner. Use them to help you write a plan for your own story.

Prompts

★ Decide whether you are going to write your story from Hannah's or John's point of view.

★ Think about where detail could be added.

★ Think about where you could use dialogue.

★ Make a list of some interesting descriptive words you could use in your story.

⑤ Write a story 3

Read the prompts with your partner. Use them and the Word bank below to help you write your story.

Prompts

★ Write from Hannah's or John's point of view. Use the first person and past tense.

★ Start a new paragraph every time you begin a new piece of action.

★ Show how characters are feeling by describing how they behave.

★ Try using interesting adverbs to begin sentences.

★ Add dialogue to give new information and to show what the characters are thinking. Try using words other than 'said' to introduce dialogue.

★ Use the map to help you describe the setting.

Word bank

Adverbs

warily	curiously	cautiously	stealthily

Alternatives for 'said'

whispered	murmured	hissed	sighed	mumbled

① Write 2

With your partner, read the Top Tips for improving the newspaper article.

Top Tips

⭐ The standfirst should be interesting. Think about how you can grab your readers' attention.

⭐ The lead paragraph should answer the questions: *Who? What? Where? When?* and *Why?*

⭐ Delete any words which have been used more than once and use synonyms to replace them, e.g. *strange* could be replaced with *unusual, unexpected, puzzling, mystifying* or *bizarre*.

⭐ Make sure each sentence makes a point. If you think a sentence is just repeating information, take it out.

⭐ Where appropriate, use a clause to add extra information – it will keep the number of words down.

Try to use some of the words in the Word bank in your article.

Word bank

distressed   fled   trembling   terrifying

extraordinary   sensational

② Deconstruction 3

Read these notes with your partner and use them to write your own entry for 'This Summer in History'.

Year: 1865

Where: The Matterhorn, a mountain in the Swiss Alps

Height: 14,690 ft

Event: First ascent of the Matterhorn by Edward Whymper, Charles Hudson, Lord Francis Douglas, Douglas Robert Hadow, Michel Croz, Peter and Peter Taugwalder (father and son).

Edward Whymper led the group. Tragedy struck as the men descended the mountain and four men died.

Sugarcane Juice

Reading

1 **Daily log**

Take turns to read the questions below and discuss the answers with your partner.

A How does Hamid get stuck on the bus?

B What do you think sugarcane juice tastes like?

C How do you think Hamid felt when he found out he was stuck on the bus?

D What do you think will happen next?

② Grammar: nouns and pronouns

Take turns to read a sentence each in this passage.

For Hamid, revving engines sounded sweeter than music, and diesel fumes smelled better than flowers. His heart thrilled to the hustle and bustle of street sellers, the comings and goings of passengers. He saw people from every corner of Pakistan: tribesmen from the north, children of all ages, wedding parties…and the buses! Gorgeously painted in rainbow colours – gaudy, tasselled and tinselled. Once they left the station the buses picked up speed, thundering towards Islamabad, Karachi, Faisalabad and other towns.

Discuss which words in the passage are:

A **Proper nouns** – names of particular places, people or things, e.g. *Africa, Jenny, Blackpool Tower*.

B **Pronouns** – words that can replace common and proper nouns, e.g. *he, her, him, it, their, they, them*.

③ Read and compare

Take turns to read a paragraph. Work together to add words and phrases about the settings to your Settings collector. Discuss the similarities and differences between the settings.

A

In the bus station

Hamid thought the bus station was the best place in the world. For him, revving engines sounded sweeter than music, and diesel fumes smelled better than flowers. His heart thrilled to the hustle and bustle of street sellers, the comings and goings of passengers. He saw people from every corner of Pakistan: tribesmen from the north, children of all ages, wedding parties…and the buses! Gorgeously painted in rainbow colours – gaudy, tasselled and tinselled.

B

Inside the bus

"Stop, Uncle, stop!" shouted Hamid, but the bus was ancient and it groaned and creaked like an old person in pain, so the driver couldn't hear him. The bus lurched and swayed under its load of passengers, goats, chickens and baskets of vegetables and fruit. Hamid looked around helplessly. The interior was festooned with tinsel, shiny bunting and mirrors. The ceiling was painted like the night sky, with stars and a full moon, and there were vases of plastic flowers stuck to the sides. The flowers nodded busily.

④ Character fact file

Take turns to read this letter from Hamid to his cousin.
Use it to find additional information about Hamid to write in
your fact file.

Dear Imran,

It was fun visiting you in the countryside. I've been helping
father every day after school and now he allows me to make
the sugarcane juice. I have to push the sugarcane through a
special mangle, which squeezes all the juice out. I am not so
good at it, yet. You have to be very strong. I am playing cricket
near our house in the evenings so I will get stronger at bowling
and batting, at least!

I had a terrible day last week. I was on one of the buses
as usual, selling juice, when it started up and drove out of
the bus station without me realising. The bus swung about,
chickens squawked and I fell over and spilled sugarcane juice
everywhere by accident! The people in the bus were really
grumpy. They shouted and called me bad names. I felt so
small and was concerned that I would get into trouble, but
the driver was very kind. He got me off the bus and gave me
money to get home.

I was in the middle of nowhere, on the side of a dusty road. I worried that my father would think I'd run away or got lost and he would tell me off for wasting my time and spilling the juice. But luckily a bus came and the driver knew my father, so he took me back to the bus station for free. Father was a bit cross but he smiled as he called me a silly goat, so I knew he was glad I was safe.

Your cousin,
Hamid

Writing

(1) What if not...?

Take turns to read the What if not...? questions. Discuss them with your partner.

A What if not *kind*? What if *the bus driver were cross, or mad, or mean*?

B What if not *safe*? What if *the bus journey was on a dangerous road*?

C What if not *Timarpur*? What if *the bus was going somewhere else*?

② Build a sentence

Take turns to read these sentences.

Hamid's eyes grew wide as he watched the villages flash by. The ancient bus spluttered and wheezed like an unfit runner as it blasted out black smoke from its exhaust. The bus rolled and weaved unsteadily as it swung around each sharp corner. Hamid was mesmerised by the jiggling chicken heads and swaying tinsel inside the bus as he clung desperately on to the handrail.

Text by Charlotte Raby

Now write four sentences of your own about the bus.

★ Start with Hamid looking out of the bus – what can he see?

★ Use a simile to describe how the bus moves.

★ Use accurate verbs to describe how the bus weaves all over the road.

★ Describe the inside of the bus to show how its movement affects its passengers and cargo.

③ Tell a story

Find the route on the map for the bus that Hamid is stuck on. Tell your partner about the journey. Remember to use accurate words to describe the perils on the way. Make it seem exciting and dangerous!

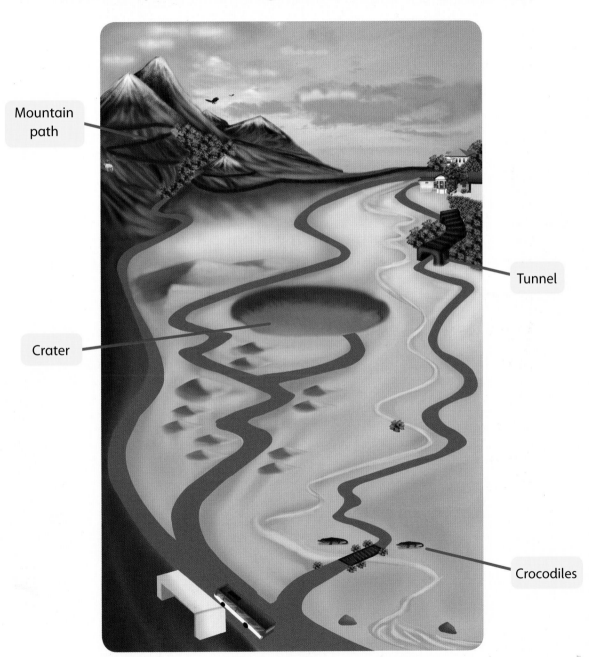

Mountain path

Tunnel

Crater

Crocodiles

(4) **Build an episode 3**

Take turns to read the episode a paragraph at a time. Use these questions to help you evaluate the writing.

A Does the episode continue on from Hamid getting stuck on the bus?

B Is there a good reason why he can't get off?

C Are the perils exciting? Do they seem dangerous?

D Is the bus described well? In what way?

(5) **Write a story 1**

Decide with your partner what will happen at the different stages of your story. Use the questions below to help you.

Build up

Why is Hamid stuck on the bus?

Problem 1

What is the first danger?

Problem 2

What is the second danger?

What does Hamid do to save the passengers and the bus?

Resolution

Where do the bus and its passengers end up?

Write a plan in your Daily log.

⑥ Write a story 3

Use these ideas to help you write your story.

★ Start off with a description of the bus as Hamid realises he is stuck on it.

★ Make the bus into another character – use similes and metaphors to describe the different parts of it.

★ Use accurate, exciting verbs to make the action seem real.

★ Use dialogue when someone is giving commands.

★ End your episode in a way that means the story can continue in the next episode.

① Change it!

Take turns to read through this section of the film critic's review. Think about how you can change it so it persuades the reader *not* to see the film.

> *VIPER!* is highly recommended for cinema-goers looking for thrills, gripping action and heart-in-mouth suspense. But beware: if you're easily scared you'd better stay at home, because this film will have you on the edge of your seat, from the breathtaking opening action right up until the final dramatic twist.
>
> *VIPER!* – don't miss it, or you'll regret it!

Talk with your partner and decide which of these persuasive techniques to use.

⭐ Use negative words like these to make the film sound boring, dull or unbelievable: *daft, stupid, unrealistic, tedious, lifeless, appalling, awful, dreadful.*

⭐ Use emotive language like this to make the reader feel negative about the film: *ridiculous, childish, silly, only an idiot would enjoy it.*

⭐ Appeal to the reader at the end with a question such as: *VIPER! – why would you waste your time and money?*